Survival Stories

Polar
Survival Stories

Cynthia O'Brien

Lerner Publications • Minneapolis

Copyright © 2026 by Lerner Publishing Group, Inc.

All rights reserved. International copyright secured. No part of this book may be reproduced, stored in a retrieval system, or transmitted in any form or by any means—electronic, mechanical, photocopying, recording, or otherwise—without the prior written permission of Lerner Publishing Group, Inc., except for the inclusion of brief quotations in an acknowledged review.

Lerner Publications Company
An imprint of Lerner Publishing Group, Inc.
241 First Avenue North
Minneapolis, MN 55401 USA

For reading levels and more information, look up this title at www.lernerbooks.com.

Main body text set in Adrianna Regular.
Typeface provided by Chank.

Library of Congress Cataloging-in-Publication Data

Names: O'Brien, Cynthia (Cynthia J.), author.
Title: Polar survival stories / Cynthia O'Brien.
Description: Minneapolis, MN : Lerner Publications, 2026. | Series: Searchlight books. Survival stories | Includes bibliographical references and index. | Audience: Ages 8-11 | Audience: Grades 4-6 | Summary: "What would you do if you were lost in the Arctic? Read about survival stories in polar conditions, including a polar bear attack and a plane malfunction over a frozen lake"— Provided by publisher.
Identifiers: LCCN 2024040418 (print) | LCCN 2024040419 (ebook) | ISBN 9798765669143 (library binding) | ISBN 9798765684788 (paperback) | ISBN 9798765680735 (epub)
Subjects: LCSH: Survival—Polar Regions—Juvenile literature. | Arctic regions—Juvenile literature.
Classification: LCC GF86 .O35 2026 (print) | LCC GF86 (ebook) | DDC 613.6/90998—dc23/eng/20241118

LC record available at https://lccn.loc.gov/2024040418
LC ebook record available at https://lccn.loc.gov/2024040419

Manufactured in the United States of America
1 – CG – 7/15/25

Table of Contents

Introduction
EXTREME COLD SURVIVAL . . . 4

Chapter 1
THE BIG FREEZE . . . 6

Chapter 2
EXTREME NORTH . . . 10

Chapter 3
DANGEROUS ENCOUNTERS . . . 16

Chapter 4
ON THE ICE . . . 22

Glossary • 30
Learn More • 31
Index • 32

Introduction

EXTREME COLD SURVIVAL

In 1972, Marten Hartwell was flying his plane to Yellowknife, Canada. The weather was bad, and Hartwell had flown off course. He checked his chart to see where he was. At that moment, his plane crashed into an Arctic hillside. Hartwell was injured and had little food. His only shelter was a tent made from sleeping bags. After four weeks, a plane picked up a signal from Hartwell's beacon. He was rescued on December 8, 1972.

The Arctic region surrounds the North Pole. Antarctica is around the South Pole. The Poles are cold year-round, and fierce storms are common. There are few or no people living in many parts of these regions. Polar visitors must be prepared. They should dress warmly. They will be far from help. They should bring shovels and other tools for hunting and making shelters.

The seas around Antarctica are freezing cold.

THE BIG FREEZE

At the North Pole temperatures can be -40°F (-40°C) in the winter. Indigenous peoples have lived in the Arctic for thousands of years. Skills such as hunting, making tools, and building shelters have helped them survive. The South Pole is even colder. Temperatures can fall to -76°F (-60°C) in winter. No one lives in Antarctica all the time.

The ice on a frozen lake in the Arctic is strong enough to land a plane on.

Off Course

Bob Gauchie was flying his plane during a snowstorm when he was forced to land on a frozen Arctic lake. He was lost and his plane was out of fuel. For fifty-eight days, Gauchie used the plane as a shelter. On April 1, 1967, he saw a plane fly overhead and lit two flares. The plane landed nearby and took Gauchie to safety.

Stranded

Ada Blackjack was stranded on Wrangel Island in the Arctic. She was with a group of four men. They had arrived on the island in 1921. By early 1923, supplies had run out. Three of the men left to find help. They did not return. The remaining man died, and Blackjack was left alone. She taught herself to hunt. Blackjack caught seals, foxes, and birds. She made a stove from cans and sewed warm clothes from animal skins. A ship finally rescued Blackjack that September. She had survived on the island for two years.

Ada Blackjack and her son in November 1923

Survival Tip

Surviving the cold requires a lot of energy. Polar explorers plan what food to take with them. The food must be high in calories but light enough to carry.

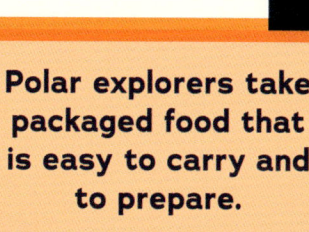

Polar explorers take packaged food that is easy to carry and to prepare.

Chapter 2

EXTREME NORTH

The Arctic is a vast area of ice and snow. The seas around it are covered with ice. People should bring emergency supplies including water and tools. These will help them survive. However, if disaster strikes, people need to call for rescue.

Rescues in the Arctic can be difficult. The harsh climate and bad weather make it hard to find people. It can be impossible for ships to break through the sea ice. Blizzards and snowstorms stop airplanes and helicopters from flying and landing safely.

AN ICEBREAKER SHIP CLEARS A PATH THROUGH THE FROZEN ARCTIC OCEAN.

Snowmobiles can travel over ice and snow.

Out of Fuel

In 2016, Pauloosie Keyootak lost his way in a snowstorm. Keyootak was in Nunavut in northern Canada with his son and nephew. The group was traveling by snowmobile. When the storm stopped, Keyootak knew they were lost. They were almost out of fuel. They didn't have a phone to call for help.

Keyootak used a knife to build a snow shelter. The others caught a caribou for food. They had a camp stove to heat water for tea. After eight days, the fuel and food ran out. Luckily, a rescue team had spotted snowmobile tracks. The rescuers followed the tracks and found Keyootak and his family.

Survival Tip

Polar travelers need polar tents, snow shovels, and warm, waterproof clothes. They should carry satellite phones or other devices that work in remote places.

Polar tents are light to carry and quick to put up.

Trapped in the Ice

A fall into an ice-covered stream nearly cost Anna Bågenholm her life. In 1999, Bågenholm was skiing in the Kjolen Mountains in Norway. She lost control and crashed into a frozen stream. She broke through the ice and started to sink, but her friends held on to her legs. They called for help.

The Kjolen Mountains are in Narvik, Norway.

A rescue helicopter took Bågenholm to the hospital.

Bågenholm's head and body were trapped under thick ice. Luckily, her head was in an air pocket, so she could breathe. It took a rescue team eighty minutes to free Bågenholm from the ice. Bågenholm suffered from severe hypothermia. At the hospital, the doctors slowly warmed her body. It took many months for Bågenholm to recover. Eventually, she returned to normal life and even started skiing again.

Chapter 3

DANGEROUS ENCOUNTERS

Most animals stay away from people. Polar animal attacks are rare, but they can be dangerous. The Arctic is home to many creatures, including polar bears. Polar bears can weigh as much as 1,600 pounds (720 kg). They can grow up to 7 feet (2 m) tall. Polar bears mainly eat seals, but they may attack people.

Antarctica's wildlife include animals such as penguins, whales, and seals. The animals live in the icy seas and around the coasts.

POLAR BEARS TRAVEL LONG DISTANCES ACROSS THE ICE.

Lucky Escape

In 2013, Matt Dyer was hiking with a group in the Torngat Mountains in northeastern Canada. Polar bears had been seen in the area. On the second day, a polar bear came close to their camp site. The hikers set off flares to scare it away.

That night, Dyer was asleep in his tent. He woke to see a shadow over the tent. It was a polar bear. The bear grabbed Dyer and started to drag him away. Rich Gross was the group's leader. He fired a flare. Right away, the bear dropped Dyer. It moved away, but did not go far. Gross fired another flare that landed near the bear's feet. The bear ran off and disappeared. The other hikers had already called for help. A helicopter arrived and took Dyer to a hospital.

Matt Dyer before the polar bear attack.

Survival Tip

Carry flares and noisemakers to scare off polar bears. Put an electric fence around your campsite. Move to a different campsite if a bear is spotted nearby.

A sign warns that polar bears may be in the area.

19

Seal Attack!

Leopard seals are predators that hunt penguins, birds, and other seals. They rarely attack humans. In 1985, Gareth Wood and two other explorers had completed a trip to explore the South Pole. The ship that would have taken them home had sunk. The men were stuck in Antarctica for a second winter.

GARETH WOOD WORKING OUT A ROUTE ON A MAP

During the second winter, the group went for a hike. They crossed a frozen bay. No one noticed a leopard seal under the ice. As Wood stepped over a thin crack, the seal leapt upwards. The animal bit into Wood's leg. It started pulling him into the water. Wood's friends kicked the seal's head with their spiky crampons. The seal let go. Then it pounced and bit Wood again. The others kept kicking. Finally, the seal slipped into the sea. Wood was able to escape.

Leopard seals hunt in the seas around Antarctica.

Chapter 4

ON THE ICE

Antarctica's nickname is The Ice. It is the coldest place on the planet and one of the driest. Winds can reach speeds of 199 miles (327 km) per hour. Most of the land is covered in thick ice sheets. There are mountains, volcanoes, and valleys underneath the ice.

No one lives in Antarctica their whole lives. People come to explore and study. Scientists visit for months or a year at a time.

Antarctica's mountains are covered in ice and snow.

Lost and Found

Early polar explorers used dog sleds to travel. Today, most people use vehicles like snowmobiles. In 1989, Keizo Funatsu and five others decided to cross Antarctica like the old explorers.

Near the end of the journey, the team set up camp for the night. Funatsu got up to feed the dogs during the night. Suddenly a blizzard hit. Funatsu could not find his way back to camp. He dug into the ground to make a shelter. After hours in the shelter, the storm had not stopped. Funatsu heard people calling his name. As they came closer, he crawled out and walked toward the sounds.

Sled dogs are strong, and can run over long distances.

Survival Tip

Snow shelters protect from the cold. They can be dug in a pile of snow or in the ground. Shelters can be made by building walls using snow and ice.

Polar travelers should bring a shovel as part of their kit.

Shackleton's ship became trapped in ice.

A Sunken Ship

For nine months, explorer Ernest Shackleton and his crew were trapped aboard their ship. The *Endurance* was stuck in the ice off the coast of Antarctica. When the ice began to crush the ship, Shackleton ordered everyone off. The ship sank soon after.

The men camped on the ice for months. In April 1916, the ice started to break up. At last the men could leave. They set out in their lifeboats. After a week, they reached an island called Elephant Island. Shackleton and a small group left to find help. Weeks later, they reached a whaling station over 800 miles (1,300 km) away. The men on Elephant Island were finally rescued in August 1916. In 2022, a search team found the sunken *Endurance*.

The men stayed on Elephant Island when Shackleton went for help.

Cracks in the Ice

Douglas Mawson wanted to map part of Antarctica. In November 1912, he and two others set out on their trip. They had two sleds and twelve dogs to pull them. A month later, tragedy struck. One man plunged into a deep crevasse. Six dogs and most of the supplies were lost with him. Another man fell ill and died.

Mawson continued. By now all the dogs had died. Mawson had to pull his sled. He tied himself to the sled with rope.

An illustration shows Douglas Mawson on Antarctica

Scientists visit the polar regions to study and do experiments.

This saved him. Mawson fell into a crevasse. The sled caught the edge of the opening and stopped him from falling. He pulled himself out and survived the trip home.

Earth's polar areas are exciting but dangerous. These incredible stories show how determination, skill, and luck helped people survive the coldest and most remote places on the planet.

Glossary

beacon: a light or fire that acts as a signal or warning

caribou: a large North American deer

chart: a map that pilots use to find their way

crampon: a spiked attachment on footwear used for walking on ice

crevasse: a deep crack in ice

flare: a device that sends a light signal

hypothermia: a condition when the body temperature is dangerously low

Indigenous: the first people to live in a place

predator: an animal that hunts other animals for food

Learn More

Britannica Kids: Arctic Regions
https://kids.britannica.com/kids/article/Arctic-Regions/352777

Eason, Sarah, *Arctic and Antarctic Survival Guide.* New York: Crabtree, 2021.

Ganeri, Anita, *Arctic and Antarctic.* New York: DK, 2022.

Kiddle: Antarctica Facts for Kids
https://kids.kiddle.co/Antarctica

National Geographic Kids: Polar Habitat
https://kids.nationalgeographic.com/nature/habitats/article/polar

O'Brien, Cynthia. *Desert Survival Stories.* Minneapolis: Lerner Publications, 2026.

Index

Antarctica, 5–6, 17, 20, 22–24, 26, 28
Arctic, 4–8, 10–11, 16

Bågenholm, Anna, 14–15
Blackjack, Ada, 8

crevasse, 28–29

Funatsu, Keizo, 24

Hartwell, Marten, 4

Keyootak, Pauloosie, 12

leopard seal, 20–21

Mawson, Douglas, 28–29

polar bear, 16–19

Shackleton, Ernest, 26–27
shelter, 4–7, 12, 24–25

Photo Acknowledgments

Image credits: Ditty_about_summer/Shutterstock, p. 5; Pi-Lens/Shutterstock, p. 7; Artem.G/New York Times/Public Domain/Wikipedia, p. 8; incamerastock/Alamy, p. 9; maks ph/Shutterstock, p. 11; Tyler Olson/Shutterstock, p. 12; Jens Ottoson/Shutterstock, p, 13; Vichie81/Shutterstock, p. 14; Christoffer Hansen/Shutterstock, p. 15; ruek66/Shutterstock, p. 17; Associated Press/Alamy, p. 18; Karen Foley/Dreamstime, p. 19; Royal Geographic Society/Alamy, p. 20; SZakharov/Shutterstock, p. 21; Lua Carlos Martins/Shutterstock, p. 23; Dmitri Khramov/Dreamstime, p. 24; Timo Palo/Creative Commons/Wikipedia, p. 25; Pictorial Press Ltd/Alamy, p. 26; Anton_Antonov/Shutterstock, p. 27; Classic Image/Alamy, p. 28; Mozgova /Dreamstime, p. 29. Special thanks to Alamy.

Cover: Dreamstime: Jan Martin Will